I Say, See You Soon.
I Wave GOODBYE!

My Amazing Toddler Behavioral Series

An Affirmation-Themed Book For Toddlers About Saying Goodbye (Ages 2-4)

By

Suzanne T. Christian

TWORAVENS
BOOKS

Two Little Ravens
CHILDREN'S NON-FICTION BOOKS

Paperback Edition: 9781964202327
Hardcover Edition: 9781964202334
Digital Edition: 9781964202341

Published in the United States by Two Ravens Books LLC,
254 Chapman Rd, Ste 209, Newark DE 19702

'Expand the mind, free the imagination, one title at a time.'
www.tworavensbooks.com

Welcome to
"I Say, See You Soon.
I Wave Goodbye!"

This book is a heartwarming collection of easy-to-understand affirmations created especially for young children. As you turn each page together, your toddler will learn positive ways to handle separation and find comfort in the knowledge that grown-ups always come back.

Each page features bright illustrations and familiar scenarios that encourage confidence and reassurance. By making this book a staple in your reading routine, you'll gradually see your little one growing more self-assured and relaxed during goodbyes, thanks to the power of repetition.

Prepare for a nurturing journey of emotional growth, comfort, and plenty of smiles with your toddler!"

Suzanne T. Christian

Sometimes goodbye means **"I'll see you soon!"**

I give Mommy a hug,
and then I wave goodbye!

Daddy goes to work,
but he comes back to play.

My grown-ups always
come back;
I smile and wave goodbye!

Goodbye for now means hello later.

I blow a kiss when I say bye-bye.
Kisses can fly!

When my teacher says,
"See you tomorrow!"
I wave and say bye-bye.

I wave goodbye with
my hands up high!

When my grown-up leaves,
I make a funny face.
They love to see me giggle!

Grandma goes home,
but she visits me again.

I say, **"See you soon,"** and wave my hands.

Sometimes I say goodbye
with a silly dance!

A big hug says,
"I love you,"
even when we say
bye-bye.

I wave goodbye!
Then I high-five myself—
so silly!

When grown-ups come back,
we share silly stories!

If I miss my friends,
I look at
our happy pictures.

I feel happy because grown-ups always come back!

I wave goodbye from the window.
Peek-a-boo!

Goodbye today,
hello tomorrow—
I wave goodbye!

I am a big kid when I say,
"See you soon!"

I say,
"Bye-bye, see you soon!"
and blow a big kiss.

I Say, See You Soon.

I Wave
Goodbye!

The End!

My Amazing Toddler Behavioral Series

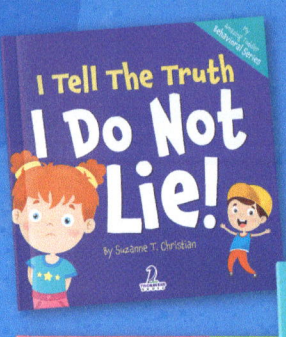

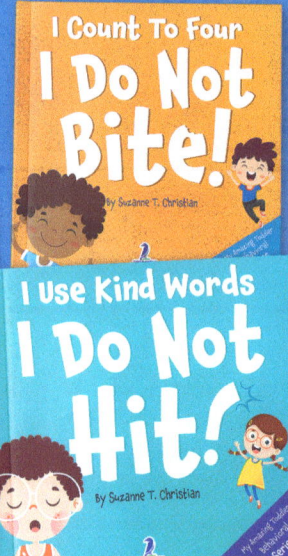

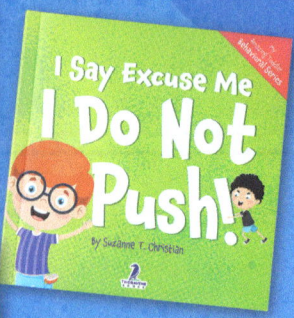

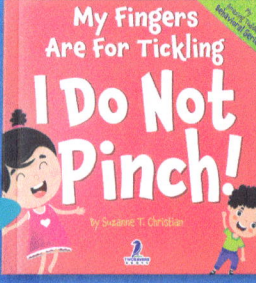

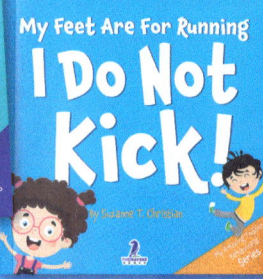

Check Out
Suzanne T. Christian's beloved series
'My Amazing Toddler Behavioral Series'.
Young readers are sure to enjoy!

Two Little Ravens

CHILDREN'S NON-FICTION BOOKS

Dear Amazing Reader,

Thank you for diving into **I Say, See You Soon. I Wave Goodbye!** with me. If this book touched your heart or made a difference for a young reader, I'd be grateful if you could share your thoughts in a review. Your feedback inspires my future work and helps others discover the magic within these pages.

I'd love to hear from you directly if you have suggestions or ideas for improving the book. Please feel free to reach out to me at **suzanne.christian@tworavensbooks.com.** Your voice counts, and I cherish it deeply.

With heartfelt gratitude,